Glimpses of God

Prayer for young adults

Raphael Appleby

First published in 1993 by
KEVIN MAYHEW LTD
Rattlesden
Bury St Edmunds
Suffolk IP30 0SZ

Front cover photograph © Heather Angel.

ISBN 086209 199 3

Typesetting & Page Creation by Anne Haskell
Cover Design by Juliette Clarke
and Graham Johnstone

Printed and bound in Great Britain.

CONTENTS

Chapter One

WHY PRAY?

Prayer is for everyone. Many people can remember the simple 'God bless Mum and Dad' formula that they were taught in childhood. Many more have cried out in desperation, 'God, please help me.' But the reality of prayer is the deep need all human beings have to find answers to the important questions of life: 'Why am I here?' 'What is the point of my life?' and so on. We can argue them out with our heads, but prayer joins both head and heart, making sense out of those deep feelings of hope and fear, of despair and love, of longing and contentment.

What Prayer Is

Someone once described the experience of going to see a most depressing film, so depressing that when she came out of the cinema she felt really miserable, as if she herself had experienced what it was like to be thoroughly bored with life, even to wanting to die. But as she walked down the street she told herself that it was only a film, and that she must not let it get to her in such a depressing way. After all, she thought, as she looked at the clouds racing by and felt the wind on her cheek, she was glad to be alive. That thought made her wonder why she was glad to be alive, and she could find no immediate answer, although she was clear in her mind that, whatever the reason, she was happy to have a tomorrow to look forward to. When thinking it over later on, she realised that she had made an act of faith.

That, really, is the beginning of what we mean by faith, simply by being glad to be alive, saying yes to what my experience of life has been so far. Of course there have been ups and downs; of course there have been times when I might truly have wished I was dead or had not been born, but if, after deep, calm reflection, I can truly say that I am glad to have been given life, glad that I am alive and have a future to look forward to, whatever it might be, then I am a person of faith.

This is not, of course, to question the faith of those who, after a long and fulfilled life, look forward to death as the way to a new and better one. But for us, at an earlier stage, love of life is the beginning of faith.

Then, of course, other questions follow. Why am I glad? Where did my life come from? Has it a purpose or a meaning? Is there a God? Any serious attempt to answer these or similar questions is really the beginning of prayer, for prayer means essentially being engaged on a search for meaning in my life. Yes, a search for meaning, because if there is a God then God is the meaning of my life and a search for meaning is a search for God. Whatever I decide is the meaning of my life can probably be called my God or gods.

Christianity claims to be a revealed religion. In other words, it believes that God has revealed himself to his creation, first of all through his chosen people, and finally through Jesus Christ, his Son. So christians believe that through a study of the life and teachings of Jesus, to be found in the Bible and interpreted by the church he founded, it is possible to discover something about God, something of his nature, of his purpose in creating men and women, of the meaning of the individual lives of each one of us.

So christianity is of great importance. One of the most significant beliefs of christianity is that God has made his dwelling place within us: *and we shall come to him and make our home with him* (Jn 14:23). So the search for God or for meaning in our lives has to take place not only in the teachings of christianity but also in the depths of our own hearts.

That searching into the depths of our hearts we call prayer. But there is no need to be alarmed. Searching never starts at a deep level and any attempt to talk to God, to listen to him, to think about him, however trivial it may seem, is to pray.

For christianity, although it is a revealed religion with its own history, is also a religion that claims to live with the life of the Holy Spirit, the Spirit promised by Jesus: *when the Spirit of truth comes he will lead you to the complete truth* (Jn 16:13). Paul tells us that *the Spirit of God has made his home in you* (Romans 8:9) and prayer, in a way, is an attempt to make sense of, almost to verify, that claim. Yet prayer is not something magical, some illuminating experience or comfortable feeling, although it can include these. Prayer is a search for meaning, a journey towards the God who has promised us his love, and like all journeys it has its ups and downs, its good times and its hard times, but if it is true that there is a God who made us because he loved us, then the search for that God is the most worthwhile search there is.

WHAT IS THE POINT OF PRAYER?

Many people will say that prayer is not all that necessary. That the most important response to life is to live it fully, as well as one can, and not to spend much time reflecting on its deeper meanings. A famous Greek philosopher once said, 'the unexamined life is not worth living,' and to refuse even to attempt to search into one's heart and experience to try and make some sense of one's life does seem a strange choice, rather like living in a garden and never even peeping over the garden wall.

There is an interesting passage in the *Upanishads* where the writer is describing the experience of the first human person to discover that he or she is a human being, with the ability to reflect on their own experience, to say, 'Gosh! I am a human being'. The first response was: 'Verily, he was alone and he was afraid.' That passage has something in common with the account of the Fall of Adam and Eve at the beginning of the book of Genesis. As soon as Adam and Eve had eaten the apple we read that *they realised they were naked*

(Gen 3:7) and later on that *they hid from Yahweh God* (3:8). So, in order to hide their nakedness, *they sewed fig leaves together* (3:7). Perhaps, like the person in the *Upanishads*, the nakedness they discovered in themselves was the nakedness of being alone and afraid.

For Adam and Eve the discovery of their own solitariness was immediate and traumatic. For most human beings the same discovery is slow and gradual, coming during the years of adolescence, with that uncertainty of who we are, of how we relate to other people, of what we are going to do with our lives, of whether or not we shall be a success, of whether or not, indeed, people can really like us just as we are. It is a period of uncertainty and it does not easily go away. Adam and Eve made themselves fig leaves to hide their own vulnerability: so, perhaps, do we, although our fig leaves are not made of green leaves. Rather they consist of anything we can use to protect that uncertain self from too much exposure to the outside world So we may use clothes, possessions, popularity, success, eccentricity, anything that we can hide behind, anything to help us cope with the burden of wondering if we are liked or even accepted by the people we admire and respect. Like Adam and Eve in their fig leaves and hiding from Yahweh God *among the trees of the garden* (Gen 3:8), we too are unfree people, unfree because we are so often alone and afraid.

How is it possible to become free? How can we become confident, free to be ourselves, no longer needing to hide? Probably with the experience of being loved, of knowing that we are loved no matter what we do, no matter what sort of person we are. The assurance of that sort of unconditional love can help us to come out of the trees, free to be ourselves. And so the young man or woman, whatever language he or she may use to describe it, is probably craving to be loved, to be fully accepted, to belong unconditionally.

This, I should want to suggest, is where prayer comes in. For prayer is a search for a God who claims that he loves us, a God who *loved the world so much that he gave his only Son . . . so that through him the world might be saved* (Jn 3: 16,17), a God who *loved us first* (1 Jn 4:19). It is easy, perhaps, to accept, even believe, this with our heads. Not so easy to know it with our hearts, for if we did truly know it we should no longer be afraid to be ourselves. If we knew with confidence that God loves us just as we are we should no longer be afraid of failure, no longer feel threatened by other people's criticisms, no longer even feel so dissatisfied and unforgiving with ourselves.

Jesus promised that he and the Father would *make our home* within us (Jn 14:23). Prayer is the attempt to make contact with the God who dwells in our hearts, the God who professes to love us. Prayer, if persevered with, can develop a relationship with the God who told us *you are my friends* (Jn 15:14) and, like all friendships, all relationships, this one needs time, perseverance, generosity and honesty. But, unlike human friendships, this one is based on the love of God that never changes, never diminishes, never gives up on us. Prayer can help us experience that love.

A FURTHER REASON FOR PRAYING

Christianity is not simply an assurance of salvation. Belief in God, acceptance of the gift of faith, carries with it also a part in the mission of Christ, in the building of his kingdom, a responsibility *to be my witnesses . . . to the ends of the earth* (Acts 1:8). Such a task invites us to look again at how Christ carried out his mission, how he coped with the hardships, the disappointments, the failures that accompanied him on his way. For his journey was a hard and unrewarding one. Constantly he was faced with people who could not or would not understand him and, as scripture reminds us, he was *one who has been tempted in every way that we are* (Hebrews 4:15). As we read through the gospels we can find him saddened, experiencing a sense of failure (John 6:64-71); we find him angry (Luke 19:45), in tears over Jerusalem and over Lazarus (Lk 19:41 and John 11:33); we find him tired and thirsty (Jn 4:6), and perhaps above all we find him troubled in spirit (Lk 12:32) and afraid (Mark 14:33).

How did Jesus cope with all this pain and struggle? The answer is: he prayed. The gospels are full of references to Jesus and prayer but perhaps the most striking example is found in the garden of Gethsemane. Here we find Jesus almost at the end of his tether. He knows what his enemies will do to him, he is about to lose all his friends and supporters who will run away, and so he prays: *My Father, if it is possible, let this cup pass me by. Nevertheless, let it be as you, not I, would have it* (Mt 26:39). He prays, and his prayer is heard. We find him rising up from his prayer, still faced with the same agonies and fears, but Jesus can face them with calm courage, a serenity that is with him all the way to the cross.

What has happened? Jesus prayed that he might discover the power of God within him, that power which would enable him to fulfil his mission, to complete his offering of himself in love, to be our saviour. Because he was fully human he needed to pray, needed to discover with his heart as well as with his head, that he had been given the spirit and power of God

And so it is with us. Christ's mission was to make the world *holy and acceptable to God* (1 Peter 2:5) and through our baptism as christians we have been called, invited, to share in that same mission, called, as Peter tells us, to be *the holy priesthood that offers the spiritual sacrifices which Jesus Christ has made acceptable to God*. But it is not easy to be a holy priesthood, not easy to do all that we do in accordance with God's will rather than our own, not easy to act always with a generous and forgiving heart. There is so much selfishness in our lives, so much boredom, frustration, loneliness, weariness of body and spirit. There are so many siren voices telling us that generosity is foolishness, that our own pleasure is the only worthwhile goal, that prayer and things of the spirit are simply a morbid waste of time.

So, like Jesus, we need to pray. We need to discover with our hearts that we, too, have the spirit and power of God within us. Prayer it is that can help us know that we are loved, know that we have been chosen, know that we matter to God, know that we belong to him and have our place in his plan for all of creation. Prayer can bring us to God.

HOW TO PRAY

Praying alone

Prayer is searching for God, communicating with God, listening to God, talking to God, being with God, experiencing God, experiencing being fully alive. It is all about relating to God, growing in friendship with God, letting God work in us, discovering the power and love of God within us. So the most intimate form of prayer is probably found when we pray alone. In its most basic form prayer is simply acknowledging the presence of God, responding to the cry of the psalmist: *Be still, and know that I am God* (Ps 45). So the simplest and most natural way of praying is to do just that, to be still, to centre on the stillness within our hearts where God is. Remember that we have his promise: *we shall come to him and make our home with him* (Jn 14:23), and we learn from the experience of the prophet Elijah that God was not in the wind, nor the earthquake, nor the fire, but in *the sound of a gentle breeze* (I Kings 19:13). To hear such a gentle sound requires stillness, silence, concentration.

None of this is easy. We tend nowadays to be noisy people living in a noisy, restless world and

God in his gentleness is neither noisy nor restless. But there is further evidence from scripture about where we can find God. When Moses was told by God to tell the children of Israel that he, Moses, was to lead them out of Egypt, he naturally asked God what his name was, *what am I to tell them*? And God replied, *I am who I am . . .* tell them *I Am has sent me to you* (Exodus 3:14). In a sense God is telling us, quite simply, that God is. We find that difficult because we find the present moment hard to grasp. So much of our time we are planning for the future, or thinking about the past, or daydreaming about never-never land, while simply being in the present moment doesn't make a lot of sense to us. Except, occasionally, when we are stirred to our depths by a beautiful sunset, or a magical moment of beauty, when we want time to stand still. Sometimes such moments can be called experiences of God, for God is in the present moment and if we can truly experience it we can truly experience God. So many people have known moments of peace, moments of joy, moments of certainty, when they have known that they were close to God even if they were never able to talk about it. Such moments are important because, in the end, God can only be truly known by the heart.

Some ways of praying alone

A wise Benedictine abbot once said 'pray as you can, not as you can't,' and people with different temperaments, different experiences, will want to pray in widely differing ways. As long as the one who prays is truly seeking God, then the prayer will be real prayer, no matter what form it takes.

Prayer of stillness
This is the most natural prayer of all, in some ways, just being in the presence of God. Find a quiet place when you have some time to spare. Put yourself in a comfortable yet concentrated posture, either sitting upright in a chair with your feet on the ground, or lying on the floor, or sitting on the floor with your back against something firm, or indeed any posture you find comfortable, providing your spine is upright. The upright spine is necessary for peaceful concentration for any reasonable length of time.

Then take time to relax your body and quieten your mind and imagination. Start with your toes and concentrate on all the parts of your body in turn, gently relaxing each part so there is no tension or stiffness in your body. This may take a while, and may sometimes be next to impossible. When that happens, do not worry. Simply offer to God your tensions, your rigidity, your over-active mind. To quieten your mind and imagination try and make an inward journey into the quiet depths, or try concentrating on something simple, such as anything you can hear. When you are reasonably quiet and relaxed concentrate peacefully on your breathing. Breath, in the scriptures the same word as spirit and life, is the sign of God's life-giving spirit in us. Just breathe quietly knowing that you are in the presence of God, that he is within you and around you and that his love sustains you.

When your mind wanders, quietly return to the still centre. Sometimes it helps to breathe a quiet word or phrase, *Lord Jesus* or *Lord, I love you.*

Praying with a mantra
This isn't some mysterious Eastern form of mysticism but a way of praying that has been a central part of the church's prayer for many centuries. *The Cloud of Unknowing*, a classical spiritual book written by an unknown English priest in the later part of the fourteenth century, tells us to *Take a short word, preferably of one syllable . . . and fix this word fast to your heart.* A favourite prayer of the Eastern Orthodox church has long been the so-called Jesus Prayer which consists of slow but constant repetition of the words: *Lord Jesus Christ, Son of the living God, have mercy on me a sinner.* For that is the essence of the use of the mantra, the slow but steady repetition of a word or phrase that keeps the attention and concentration gently but firmly on being still in the presence of God. Perhaps the best description of praying with a mantra comes from John Main's book, *Word Into Silence* (Darton, Longman & Todd): 'Sit down. Sit still and upright. Close your eyes lightly. Sit relaxed but alert. Silently, interiorly, begin to say a single word. We recommend the prayer-phrase 'maranatha'. Recite it as four syllables of equal length. Listen to it as you say it, gently but continuously. Do not think or imagine anything – spiritual or otherwise. If thoughts and images come, these are distractions at the time of

meditation, so keep returning simply to saying the word.'

Talking to God

If you are one of those people who can easily talk to God in your own words, sharing with him your feelings, your thoughts, your hopes, your fears, then you are a lucky person. For that is the heart of friendship, being able to share honestly and openly the real truth that lies deep in our hearts. So it is good to talk to God as you talk to a friend. Perhaps talking through the events and emotions of the day with him, perhaps sharing your joys and excitements with him, perhaps pouring out your worries and depressions, sometimes thanking him, sometimes praising him, sometimes just talking to him.

Jesus tells us: *I call you friends* (Jn 15:15), an invitation to share our lives with him as friend does with friend. Which means that he does not only want us to talk with him when we are feeling positive and cheerful. He wants also to hear about our hurts and failures, our moods and depressions, our bitterness and our anger. He even wants to know when we are angry with him. To learn to talk honestly to God is one of the most precious forms of prayer.

Formal prayers or other peoples' prayers

Many people find formal prayers, such as saying the *Our Father*, difficult, because it is so easy to gabble the words, to find that the prayer is over before we realised we had started it. But formal prayers are not solely for formal liturgy. What makes prayer real prayer is the desire to search for God, to want to communicate with him in some way, and the intention is much more important than the method. But formal prayers often say, with dignity and beauty, what it is we want to say to God, and, what is worth thinking about, they link our prayer with the prayer of all christians everywhere, so that whether we are saying the *Our Father*, or reciting the Divine Office, or parts of it, we are taking part in the prayer of the whole church, of the whole People of God.

Often, too, it helps to use prayers that others have written, prayers that seem to meet our need of the moment. Or to find passages of poetry or reflection that help us to move our hearts and minds towards God. Sometimes, too, when feeling empty, or in pain, or afraid, the words of a familiar prayer can be of much strength and support. Perhaps the best way to approach formal prayers is to try to find the time to say them slowly, to let the words have space, not to analyse them but to let them sink into our hearts.

Holy reading

The monastic tradition has developed a way of praying that many people who do not live in monasteries find helpful. It is based on a passage from scripture and has four parts. The first part, called, *reading*, is to read and re-read the passage slowly so that it can be properly absorbed. The second part, called *meditation*, is to work out the meaning of the passage, perhaps sometimes using a commentary, trying to discover what it is saying to me today. The third part, called *prayer*, is to talk with God about what has been read and understood. Perhaps that will mean thanking him, or asking forgiveness, or making resolutions, or praising him. The last part, called *contemplation*, involves simply waiting in silence with God. It is essentially silent, no words, just stillness. The word contemplation really means *looking at*, and it is a period in which we gently sit still and look at God: *Be still and know that I am God* (Ps 45).

One advantage of this form of holy reading is that it is easily variable. One person will spend more time on contemplation, another on talking to God, a third on the reading itself. But, as with all forms of prayer, there is no right or wrong way. *Pray as you can*. One further word may be helpful here. When meditating on a passage from scripture, some people prefer to use their imaginations to get right back into the time of the event or teaching described, to try and picture the scenery, the people, what they are wearing, perhaps to get inside one of the characters and feel what it was like to hear what Jesus said or to see what he did. In that way it is sometimes possible to get a deep understanding and sympathy with the meaning of the passage. Another way is to relate the passage directly to oneself. Instead of getting back to the past this method brings Jesus immediately to the present, so that we imagine

Jesus talking to me, here and now, or the passage of scripture being directly addressed to me personally. Sometimes it can help actually to write the passage out, inserting my own name into the relevant places: for example, *Before the world was made, he chose us, chose us in Christ* (Eph 1:4) becomes *Before the world was made, he chose Raphael, chose me in Christ.*

Praying with others

While it is good to pray alone it is also good to pray with others. Indeed, Christ founded a church and it is as members of his church, his body, that we call ourselves christians. The very first words of the Lord's Prayer, *Our Father*, remind us that it is together we call upon God. Sunday by Sunday, all over the world, christians come together to pray, to worship God, to acknowledge and celebrate their common unity as members of the Body of Christ. But there is also a place for more informal prayer together and many people find this one of the most helpful ways of praying. Coming together, sharing a faith, sharing our feelings, is a real means to growth in prayer and getting closer to God There are a number of ways in which this can be done.

Shared prayer

One simple way to pray together is to come together for a short period and invite anyone who wishes to pray aloud, asking God for whatever they want, or thanking him or praising him in their own words. There is no need for all to pray, although if there are only two people involved it helps if they both take part and truly share their prayer. Then after a little silence the prayer can be concluded with a shared *Our Father* or another suitable prayer.

A further development of shared prayer is for people to share what they are feeling, their sadnesses or upsets or pressures or fears, or indeed their joys and delights, their blessings and hopes. Then those taking part can pray for each other, asking God to help in whatever way is needed, as has been shown by what each one has shared.

Sometimes, too, it can help to take a piece of scripture or some other suitable reading, ask someone to read it aloud, spend a while reflecting on it in silence, and then share these reflections. If possible, a song or a hymn or a simple chant can bring people together and can express in prayer what people want to say to God. A guitar or a flute helps, but there are many well-known chants and refrains that do not need any accompaniment.

Prayer services
It is sometimes helpful to have a more organised form of praying together. This can be arranged in a number of different ways, but it may help to include readings, both from scripture and other sources, songs, periods of shared prayer, time for praise, time for thanksgiving, time for asking, perhaps time for healing, certainly time for silence. This last requirement, often overlooked in planning, is particularly important at all times

when people pray together. It is so necessary to listen to the Holy Spirit and that can generally best be done during a time of silence. Furthermore, a shared silence can often be a particularly rich and helpful experience of prayer.

A time for healing or reconciliation can be a most rewarding part of a prayer service. It is so necessary for us to recognise that we are part of a body, the Body of Christ, that we do hurt each other, that we have been hurt ourselves, that we do all need both reconciliation and healing. Simple ways of expressing this, perhaps, when suitable, a little sharing, and then a prayer for healing and forgiveness, are all that is needed. A way of praying for healing can be found later on in the book.

Sensitive use of the well-known Taizé chants can be most useful when planning a prayer service. They do not need accompaniment, are easily learnt, are deeply scriptural, and can help to produce an atmosphere of stillness, peace and prayer. Music does have a significant part to play in almost any prayer service, although if it is not possible to provide it the prayer can still take place with nothing lost.

Different ways of praying
This introduction on ways of praying is not meant to be exhaustive and there are many books on prayer which are well worth reading. Let it suffice to mention here a number of other ways in which people have found it possible to pray. Anthony de Mello in his book *Sadhana* provides a goldmine for

people looking for ways of praying in silence and his introduction is a most helpful account of how and why we pray. William Johnston's *Being in Love* is a comprehensive and very readable account of how to pray, with many useful suggestions of what might be done. And there are many more.

For many, many people the rosary is a most important way of praying, although not all can manage it. The quiet repetition of the Hail Marys while reflecting on the mysteries of the faith can deepen our understanding of those mysteries by a process of quiet assimilation. For others, there are times when we can best pray by going for a walk and consciously recognising God in the trees and flowers we see around us, or by listening to music that can move the heart towards its creator, or by just slowly reading a psalm and letting the words sink in, or by simply sitting still and offering to God the weariness and restlessness which makes it impossible to pray. It can also be really helpful, and can make prayer very relevant, to look at a daily paper, or watch a TV news bulletin, and reflect on what you have read or seen in the light of your own faith, perhaps asking the question, 'Where is God in all this?' Prayer is a looking for God and anything that helps us in our search for him is or can be a prayer.

HOW TO USE THIS BOOK

All prayer books are merely starting points, something to help us on our way as we try to make God a real part of our lives, or search for him deep down within us. This book is no exception. What follows are a series of prayers and reflective passages, many from scripture and a good number from other sources. They are divided into themes with a short introductory paragraph.

Prayer is often helped with something to think about and any of the passages that follow may best be used by a slow, careful reading followed by at least one or two re-readings. Many of them will then benefit from a reflection or examination of what they mean and of what they are perhaps saying to me here and now as I read them. This might well lead on to a desire to talk to God about the meaning, what is said, how it relates to me, what my next step might be. Finally, it is always best to spend at least a short time simply in stillness before the Lord, letting all that has been read, reflected on or talked about with God, sink quietly into the mind and heart, a time of simply being still with God.

Chapter Two

PRAYER

THERE are many ways of thinking about God. We must never reduce God to whatever image we may have been given in childhood. Both the scriptures and men and women of prayer give us glimpses of God's own revelation of himself. But God can never be imprisoned in a single image. Do not be afraid to follow your heart and your imagination.

GOD CALLS MOSES

Then Moses said to God, 'I am to go then to the
sons of Israel and say to them, "The God of our
fathers has sent me to you", but if they ask me
what his name is, what am I to tell them?'
And God said to Moses, 'I am who I am. This',
he added, 'is what you must say to the sons of
Israel; "I am has sent me to you".'

EXODUS 3:13-14

GOD PREPARES A BANQUET

On this mountain,
Yahweh Sabaoth will prepare for all peoples
a banquet of rich food, a banquet of fine wines,
of food rich and juicy, of fine strained wines.
On this mountain he will remove
the mourning veil covering all peoples,
and the shroud enwrapping all nations,
he will destroy Death for ever.
The Lord Yahweh will wipe away
the tears from every cheek;
he will take away his people's shame
everywhere on earth,
for Yahweh has said so.
That day, it will be said: See, this is our God
in whom we hoped for salvation;
Yahweh is the one in whom we hoped.
We exult and we rejoice
that he has saved us;
for the hand of Yahweh
rests on this mountain.

ISAIAH 25:6-10

WHO IS GOD?

Who is God, then, to love like this
   the children of the earth?

Who is God, then, to make an equal bond
   of love with us?

Who is God, then, if we, to find him,
   must know ourselves so poor?

Who is God, then, who walks beside us
   along our human ways?

Who is God, then, who does not flinch to
   take our food and drink?

Who is God, then, whom none can love,
   not loving people?

Who is God, then, who is so deeply wounded,
   when we wound men?

Who is God, then, who in his own death,
   bears us to life?

Who is God, then, who opens to us
   his joy and kingdom?

J. SERVEL

GOD NEVER ABANDONS

For Zion was saying, 'Yahweh has abandoned me,
the Lord has forgotten me.'
Does a woman forget her baby at the breast,
or fail to cherish the son of her womb?
Yet even if these forget, I will never forget you.
See, I have branded you on the palms of my hands.

ISAIAH 49:14-16

CONTEMPLATION

Now turn to contemplation. What is it? Oh, not the
popular sense of 'contemplate', which is instantly
associated with 'navel'.

Contemplation in its profound sense is just as real
as your navel but far more exciting.

The contemplative carmelite William McNamara
once called it 'a pure intuition of being,

born of love. It is experiential awareness of reality
and a way of entering into immediate communion
with reality.'

And what is reality?

'People, trees, lakes, mountains.

You can study things,

but unless you enter into this intuitive communion
   with them,

you can only know *about* them,
   you don't *know* them.

To take a long, loving look at something –
a child, a glass of wine, a beautiful meal –
this is a natural act of contemplation,
   of loving admiration.'

The problem?

'All the way through school we are taught
   to abstract;

we are not taught loving awareness.

Never have I heard contemplation more excitingly
   described:

a long loving look at the real . . .

Reality is living, pulsing people;
reality is fire and ice;
reality is the sun setting over the Swiss Alps,

a gentle doe streaking through the forest;
reality is a ruddy glass of Burgundy, Beethoven's
    Mass in D,
a child lapping a chocolate ice-cream cone;
reality is a striding woman with wind-blown hair;
reality is the risen Christ.

WALTER J. BURGHARDT *Church* Winter 1989

GOD IS ON YOUR SIDE

Yahweh your God goes in front of you
and will be fighting on your side
as you saw him fight for you in Egypt.
In the wilderness, too, you saw him:
how Yahweh carried you, as a man carries
    his child,
all along the road you travelled on the way to
    this place.

DEUTERONOMY 1:30-32

SEEKING CHRIST

Seeking you, the Christ, is discovering
that you already loved us
and we did not know it.
Through the Gospel, you enable us
to catch a glimpse of how to love you,
right into our innermost solitude.
Happy those who surrender themselves to you.
Happy those who approach you
in trust of heart,
source of serene joy.

BR ROGER OF TAIZÉ

THE DOORS OF MY HEART

The doors of my heart were so well locked,
and you, God, lying in wait in the night,
broke them open,
with the violence of your love.

On the evening wind
I hear the feet
of the Hound of Heaven,
soft and fleet,
and my heart lies still,
and does not beat.

What am I in the presence of your glory?
Nothing, if I look at my sin;
all that is, if I look at your love . . .

An empty shell; for only you,
the sea in the night,
can make sea change:
I am rich and strange,
and clothed with light.

P. GRIOLET

JESUS, THE WAY TO THE FATHER

Jesus said: 'to have seen me
is to have seen the father,
so how can you say, "let us
see the Father"? Do you
not believe that I am in the
Father and the Father in me?

JOHN 14:9-10

TO KNOW GOD

To know God is life eternal.
To know God is to know goodness;
   it is to see the beauty, of infinite love;
to see it attended with almighty power and eternal
   wisdom.
It is to see the king of heaven and earth take
   infinite delight in giving.
He is not an object of terror, but delight.
To know him therefore as he is, is to frame the
most beautiful idea in all worlds.
He delights in our happiness more than we do.
An infinite Lord, who, having all riches, honours
   and pleasures in his own hand,
is infinitely willing to give them unto me.

THOMAS TRAHERNE

IN NEED OF HELP

It is not as if we had a high priest
who was incapable
of feeling our weaknesses with us;
but we have one
who has been tempted in every way that we are,
though he is without sin.
Let us be confident, then,
in approaching the throne of grace,
that we shall have mercy from him
and find grace
when we are in need of help.

HEBREWS 4:15-16

THE KINGSHIP OF JESUS

So Pilate went back into the Praetorium
and called Jesus to him,
'Are you the king of the Jews?' he asked.
Jesus replied, 'Do you ask this of your own accord,
or have others spoken to you about me?'
Pilate answered, 'Am I a Jew?
It is your own people and the chief priests who
have handed you over to me:
what have you done?'
Jesus replied, 'Mine is not a kingdom of this world;
if my kingdom were of this world,
my men would have fought
to prevent my being surrendered to the Jews.
But my kingdom is not of this kind.'
'So you are a king then?' said Pilate.
'It is you who say it,' answered Jesus.
'Yes, I am a king.
I was born for this,
I came into the world for this:
to bear witness to the truth;
all who are on the side of truth listen to my voice.'

JOHN 18:33-37

Chapter Three

ME

SOMETIMES I wish, if only I could be like someone else, or at least someone other than the person I feel myself to be. Yet it was I who was made in the image and likeness of God: I am unique, lovable, never-to-be-repeated.

To Understand Myself

I want, by understanding myself,
to understand others.
I want to be all
that I am capable of becoming . . .
This all sounds
very strenuous and serious.
But now that I have wrestled with it,
it's no longer so.
I feel happy – deep down.
All is well.

Katherine Mansfield

Exclusively Mine

That I am a human being
I have in common with all men and women,
that I see and hear
and eat and drink
I share with all animals.
But that I am I is exclusively mine,
and belongs to me
and to nobody else,
to no other person,
nor to an angel nor to God,
except inasmuch as I am one with him.

Meister Eckhart

Don't Change

I was a neurotic for years. I was anxious and
    depressed and selfish. Everyone kept telling me
    to change.

I resented them, and I agreed with them,
    and I wanted to change, but simply couldn't,
    no matter how hard I tried.

What hurt the most was that, like the others,
    my best friend kept insisting that I change.
    So I felt powerless and trapped.

Then one day, he said to me, 'Don't change.
    I love you just as you are.'

Those words were music to my ears:
    'Don't change. Don't change. Don't change . . .
    I love you as you are.'

I relaxed. I came alive. And suddenly I changed!

Now I know that I couldn't really change until I
    found someone who would love me whether
    I changed or not.

Is this how you love me, God?

Anthony de Mello

THE SKIN HORSE

'Real isn't how you are made,' said the Skin Horse. 'It's a thing that happens to you. When a child loves you for a long, long time, not just to play with, but REALLY loves you, then you become Real.'

'Does it hurt?' asked the Rabbit.

'Sometimes,' said the Skin Horse, for he was always truthful. 'When you are Real, you don't mind being hurt.'

'Does it happen all at once, like being wound up,' he asked, 'or bit by bit?'
'It doesn't happen all at once,' said the Skin Horse. 'You become. It takes a long time. That's why it doesn't often happen to people who break easily, or have sharp edges, or who have to be carefully kept. Generally, by the time you are Real, most of your hair has been loved off, and your eyes drop out, and you get loose in the joints and very shabby. But these things don't matter at all, because once you are Real, you can't be ugly, except to people who don't understand.'

MARGERY WILLIAMS *The Velveteen Rabbit*

CHANGE THE WORLD
BY CHANGING ME

The Sufi Bayazid says this about himself:

I was a revolutionary when I was young and all my prayer to God was 'Lord, give me the energy to change the world'.

As I approached middle age and realized that half my life was gone without my changing a single soul, I changed my prayer to 'Lord, give me the grace to change all those who come in contact with me. Just my family and friends, and I shall be satisfied.'

Now that I am an old man and my days are numbered, my one prayer is, 'Lord, give me the grace to change myself.' If I had prayed for this right from the start I should not have wasted my life.

ANTHONY DE MELLO

MORE THOUGHTS – ON THE TUBE

Letting in depression
   is like letting the devil dance on your soul.
It gives him the freedom to prong you
   with his trident of fear, guilt and doubt.
He twists it deep within
   until you begin to believe the darkest things
     about yourself –
and the more you believe these things
   the more you become the distorted image
     that is not you.

You see, he holds up a mirror for you to see –
   and you see yourself –
but you are looking into distorting glass –
   the kind you see at fairgrounds
so although you see something that resembles you
   it is not the true you.

If you want to see the real you
   look into the eye of God –
for when you look into the eye of someone
   who loves you perfectly
the image becomes complete.

You will see your gifts as realities
and although you will see your faults
   they will not overwhelm you.
They are a small part of the whole
   and the whole is something that was created
     out of love.

A child of love should not let the devil dance on
his soul.

'I sought the Lord, and he answered me;
he delivered me from all my fears.
Those who look to him are radiant:
their faces are never covered in shame.'

PSALM 34:4-5

MARY JELF

Chapter Four

SEARCHING

WHAT AM I to do with my life? How hard it is sometimes to find the right road, to choose the right job, or the right partner. How can I know where God is leading me? How can I find God? Much searching needs to be done if I am to find where God is truly leading me, yet lead me he does.

THE LITTLE FISH

'Excuse me,' said an ocean fish.
'You are older than I, so
can you tell me where to find
this thing they call the ocean?'

'The ocean,' said the older fish, is the thing you are
in now.'
'Oh, this? But this is water. What I'm seeking
is the ocean,' said the disappointed fish
as he swam away to search elsewhere.

He came to the master in sannyasi robes. And he
spoke sannyasi language: 'For years I have been
seeking God. I have sought him everywhere that
he is said to be: on mountain peaks, the vastness of
the desert, the silence of the cloister, and the
dwellings of the poor.'

'Have you found him?' the master asked.
'No. I have not. Have you?'
What could the master say? The evening sun was
sending shafts of golden light into the room.
Hundreds of sparrows were twittering on a nearby
banyan tree. In the distance one could hear the
sound of highway traffic. A mosquito droned a
warning that it was going to strike . . . And yet this
man could sit there and say he had not found God.
After a while he left, disappointed, to search
elsewhere.

Stop searching, little fish. There isn't anything to
look *for*.
All you have to do is to *look*.

ANTHONY DE MELLO *The Song of the Bird*

THE LORD PROTECTS

The word of Yahweh was addressed to me, saying,
    'Before I formed you in the womb I knew you;
    before you came to birth I consecrated you;
    I have appointed you as prophet to the nations.'

I said, 'Ah, Lord Yahweh; look, I do not know how
    to speak: I am a child! '
But Yahweh replied,
    'Do not say, 'I am a child'.
    Go now to those to whom I send you
    and say whatever I command you.
Do not be afraid of them,
    for I am with you to protect you –
    it is Yahweh who speaks!'

JEREMIAH 1:4-8

WE ARE NO LONGER ALONE

In stillness we live
In peace we walk
Waiting for you.

In silence, we listen,
and when all is quiet
when even the breeze is calmed,
we hear your voice,
deep as earth,
deep within us,
strong as stone,
and we are no longer alone.

MARY JELF

LORD, YOU KNOW ME

O Lord, you search me and you know me,
you know my resting and my rising,
you discern my purpose from afar.
You mark when I walk or lie down,
all my ways lie open to you.

Before ever a word is on my tongue
you know it, O Lord, through and through.
Behind and before you besiege me,
your hand ever laid upon me.
Too wonderful for me, this knowledge,
too high, beyond my reach.

O where can I go from your spirit,
or where can I flee from your face?
If I climb the heavens, you are there.
If I lie in the grave, you are there.

If I take the wings of the dawn
and dwell at the sea's furthest end,
even there your hand would lead me,
your right hand would hold me fast.

If I say: 'Let the darkness hide me
and the light around me be night,'
even darkness is not dark for you
and the night is as clear as the day.

For it was you who created my being,
knit me together in my mother's womb.
I thank you for the wonder of my being,
for the wonders of all your creation.

Already you knew my soul,
my body held no secret from you
when I was being fashioned in secret
and moulded in the depths of the earth.

Your eyes saw all my actions,
they were all of them written in your book;
every one of my days was decreed
before one of them came into being.

To me, how mysterious your thoughts,
the sum of them not to be numbered!
If I count them, they are more than sand;
to finish, I must be eternal, like you.

O search me, God, and know my heart.
O test me and know my thoughts,
See that I follow not the wrong path
and lead me in the path of life eternal.

PSALM 139

SEARCH FOR THE LORD

Look, I am standing at the door, knocking.
  If one of you hears me calling
  and opens the door,
  I will come in to share his meal,
  side by side with him.

REVELATION 3: 20

A GENTLE BREEZE

Then Yahweh himself went by.
There came a mighty wind, so strong
  it tore the mountains
and shattered the rocks before Yahweh.
But Yahweh was not in the wind.
After the wind came an earthquake.
But Yahweh was not in the earthquake.
After the earthquake came a fire.
But Yahweh was not in the fire.
And after the fire there came the sound
  of a gentle breeze.
And when Elijah heard this, he covered his face
  with his cloak
and went out and stood at the entrance to his cave.

I KINGS 19: 11-13

ENLIGHTEN US

Father, we pray for guidance. It is difficult to come
to a decision. Enlighten our minds, and move our
hearts, so that we may understand better, and come
to do what seems to be right, and in accordance
with your will, in so far as we can see it. Amen.

SEARCHING FOR FREEDOM

A man who refuses to commit himself
for fear of following an insight
that cannot be mathematically verified
does *not* in fact remain free
but rather enters upon
the worst of all commitments –
that of living his life without commitment.
He tries to live as a neutral,
deciding nothing,
and that in itself is a decision.

KARL RAHNER

THE AUTHENTIC HUMAN BEING

Vatican Council II says: 'The mystery of man can
now be explained only in the mystery of God who
became man' (Gaudium et Spes, 22).
If people want to look into their own mystery – the
meaning of their pain, of their work, of their
suffering, of their hope – let them put themselves
next to Christ. If they accomplish what Christ
accomplished – doing the Father's will, filling
themselves with the life that Christ gives the
world – they are fulfilling themselves as true
human beings. If I find, on comparing myself with
Christ, that my life is the antithesis, the opposite of
his, my life is a disaster. I cannot explain that
mystery except by returning to Christ, who gives
authentic features to a person who wants to be
genuinely human.

ARCHBISHOP ROMERO (EL SALVADOR)

INVOLVED IN MANKIND

Once you associate yourself
with a human community,
whether it be a church,
a political party, or even a nation,
you are then burdened with stupidity,
with venality,
and all the faults and vices
of the men and women
who make up that particular community.
This is a problem for all of us,
because we would like
both to escape history
and to get our brothers off our back.
But we are all involved in mankind
and simply cannot take
the kind of Olympian view
of our country, our culture, our tradition,
that habitually refers to 'they'
and never to 'we'.

JOHN COGLEY

ESSENCE OF TRUE CONVERSION

When we come to God to be saved, then, I say, the
essence of true conversion is a *surrender* of oneself,
an unreserved, unconditional surrender . . . What
then is it that we who profess religion lack?
I repeat it, this: a willingness to be changed,
a willingness to suffer (if I may use such a word),
to suffer Almighty God to change us. We do not
like to let go our old selves.

JOHN HENRY NEWMAN

Chapter Five

FAITH, DOUBT & HOPELESSNESS

A T TIMES God seems far away, so far that sometimes I feel close to despair. Is it my fault or God's? At moments like this it is hard to find any hope.

IN THIS HOUR OF DESPAIR

In this hour of despair and hopelessness
I come to you for comfort;
rescue me from my despair and give me faith,
    hope and love,
else I will not be able to participate in your saving
    work in the world;
I will from weariness collapse and die.

O Lord, my God, if I in my despair
    wronged anyone,
if I let a friend down or hurt in my impatience
    those who love me –
If I have done any of these things,
then do not leave me in my guilt to endless grief.
Forgive, O Lord, forgive me and restore me to
    your love . . .

I thank you, Lord, for I know that you are at work;
you hold the whole world in your hands
    and you can change it.
I will sing your praises at all times.

ZEPHANIA KAMEETA (NAMIBIA)
An adaptation of Psalm 7

HAVE YOU GIVEN ME UP?

Have you given me up, Lord?
Are you remembering the uncountable times
    that I have failed you?
Then I am remembering your steadfast love,
    that your concern is for those
        who fail and fumble,
    that you seek to restore those
    who humbly reach out for you.

DESPAIR AND DARKNESS

O God, sometimes you seem so far away.
I cannot in this moment sense your presence
   or feel your power.

The darkness about me is stifling.
This depression is suffocating.
How long, O God, do I have to live in this void?
O God, how long?

Break into this black night, O God;
   fill in this vast emptiness.
Enter into my conflict
   lest I fall never to rise again.

I continue to trust in your ever-present love.
I shall again discover true joy
   in my relationship to you.
I will proclaim your praises, my Lord,
   for you will never let me go

PSALM 13 FROM *Psalms Now*

LIGHT IN THE DARKNESS

Lord, I am in despair. Life as I have known it is
crumbling into ruins. I have been looking for
human support and have found none. My friends
are too busy, probably with things and people of
much more importance than I. And, Lord, you do
not seem to be giving me much help either. If you
are good, please give me some light in the great
darkness which surrounds me, and give me
strength to bear my burdens which are too great
for me alone.

MICHAEL HOLLINGS

WHY AM I SO SAD?

As a desert wanderer longs for springs
    of cool water,
        so my thirsty soul reaches out for you, O God.
How I long for a deeper sense of your presence,
    for a faith that will embrace you
        without fear or doubt!
Yet while I weep in longing, people about me say,
    'If God is not dead, where is he?'

I remember so well the faith of my childhood.
How real God was to me in those days
    when I prayed and sang praises
    and listened to his word
    in the fellowship of family and friends!
Then why am I so depressed now;
Why cannot I recapture the joy and confidence
    of those years?
I remember the stories of your love
    that I had been taught;
        how merciful and all-powerful were
            your dealings
    with your children throughout history!
Yet now my heart is empty,
    and waves of doubt flood over my soul.

I pray, but the heavens, too, are empty.
It is almost as if God had forgotten all about me.
And while I struggle with the sickness of doubt,
    people about me say,
        'If God is not dead, where is he?'

O foolish heart, why do you seethe in unrest?
God has not changed;
his love for me is ever the same.
I must renew my faith in God;
I must again shout his praises
even when I don't feel his presence.
For truly he is God,
   and he is my help and my hope.

PSALM 42 FROM *Psalms Now*

HELP THOU MY UNBELIEF

I am lost!
   I am the Way.
It is so dark!
   I am the Light.
I can't believe it!
   I am the Truth.
I feel so dead!
   I am the Resurrection and the Life.
I hear what you say but I can't open up
      and believe it.
   Behold I stand at the door and knock.
   If anyone hears my voice and opens the door
      I will come in . . .
Lord, help me to open the door of my heart
      and welcome you in, I need you so much.
   With men this is impossible but with God
      all things are possible.
Lord I believe, help thou my unbelief.
Even so, come Lord Jesus.

MICHAEL HOLLINGS

EVERYTHING IS EMPTY

Lord, everything is empty and futile and there
seems no use in making an effort to keep on. I
don't know what to do when this purposelessness
engulfs me and drags me down into emptiness.
Lord, how can you be with me now; you always
seem to have known that you were doing your
Father's will. Lord, do not leave me in this
purposelessness, take away my sense of
uselessness; or do you want me to remain this way
along with the many who have to live like this
nowadays? If you do, somehow or other share the
burden of this state and help me to love those who
also suffer in this way and who do not have even
my faint glimmerings of faith and hope.
Strengthen us, dear Lord!

MICHAEL HOLLINGS

WHY HAVE YOU DESERTED ME?

When the sixth hour came
there was darkness over the whole land
    until the ninth hour.
And at the ninth hour Jesus cried out
    in a loud voice,
'Eloi, Eloi, lama sabacthani?'
which means,
'My God, my God, why have you deserted me?'

MARK 15: 33-34

WHERE ARE YOU, LORD?

'They' keep telling me that there are people who are much worse off than I am, and who have more to suffer. This is no help, for I look at all the misery and suffering there is in the world, and this makes me feel worse for there seem so few good things happening and so few people happy and successful. Most of life appears to be tragic. Where are you, Lord? Is this how you want it? If it is, why should I struggle with my gloom and try to keep going? Can you show me something to give me hope? Are you good and do you care? Your Son cared but he ended on a cross – or did he? What does 'risen from the dead' mean? Is there hope to be found in his resurrection?

MICHAEL HOLLINGS

I HAVE FAILED

I have made a mess of things. I have failed myself, my family and I've failed God. I suppose the depth and awfulness of my feelings come as much from failing myself as anything else. Why have I been such a fool? How can I ever face people? Lord, I see no end to this dark tunnel. I don't believe it's possible, but give me a glimmer of light!

MICHAEL HOLLINGS

Chapter Six

SUFFERING & SORROW

LIFE CAN be full of sorrow, the loss of a friend, the death of someone close to me, or simply the feeling of deep inadequacy or failure within myself. Yet God does offer healing, real deep healing, if we can but trust him.

IN FAILURE

God is frail.

He finds us
in failure,
and dark.

The more we fail,
the closer
we draw to him.

Failing
is the hardest gift
of all.

KATHERINE CHARNEY

EVERYTHING IS POSSIBLE

Jesus said: 'Everything is possible
for anyone who has faith.'
Immediately the father of the boy cried out,
'I do have faith. Help the little faith I have.'

MARK 9:23-24

MY SOUL IS SORROWFUL

Jesus took Peter and the two sons of Zebedee
    with him.
And sadness came over him, and great distress.
Then he said to them, 'My soul is sorrowful

to the point of death.
Wait here and keep awake with me'.
And going on a little further he fell on his face
    and prayed.
'My Father,' he said, 'if it is possible,
    let this cup pass me by.
Nevertheless, let it be as you, not I,
    would have it.'

MATTHEW 26: 37-39

WHEN UNABLE TO SLEEP

Abba, Father,
the world is so quiet.
Everyone is asleep
except me.
I worry about so many things.
Now I worry that I will still not have slept
when it is time to get up.
Help me to relax.
To put aside disturbing thoughts
and think instead of your closeness to me.
In these moments of quiet
I ask you for your Spirit,
the Spirit who brings peace and tranquillity,
to enfold me in his love,
removing all fear and anxiety,
and instilling his calmness into the very centre
of my being.

ANTHONY BULLEN *Catholic Prayer Book*

SPRING AND FALL
To a young child

Margaret, are you grieving
Over Goldengrove unleaving?
Leaves, like the things of man, you
With your fresh thoughts care for, can you?
Ah! as the heart grows older
It will come to such sights colder
By and by, nor spare a sigh
Though worlds of wanwood leafmeal lie;
And yet you will weep and know why.
Now no matter, child, the name:
Sorrow's springs are the same.
Nor mouth had, no nor mind expressed
What heart heard of, ghost guessed:
It is the blight man was born for,
It is Margaret you mourn for.

GERARD MANLEY HOPKINS

FEELING SAD AND DESPONDENT

Lord Jesus,
in your agony in the garden
you said, 'my soul is sorrowful
    to the point of death.'
I too am now feeling sad and despondent.
You know the cause.
The power of your Spirit can give me the remedy.
Heal me, Lord, of this depression.
Give me the joy and peace of knowing
that nothing in life or death
    can separate me from you.

FEELING HURT

As you were nailed to the cross, Lord Jesus,
you said: 'Father, forgive them;
they do not know what they are doing.'
You were practising what you yourself
    had preached:
'Pray for those who treat you badly.'
I feel badly done to.
I feel hurt.
I too now pray for the one who has hurt me.
While you bless this person, Lord Jesus,
remove from me all feelings of bitterness and
    anger and hurt.
Heal me of those feelings which harm only me
and instead grant me your peace.

THOSE HE HAS CHOSEN

The souls of the virtuous are in the hands of God,
no torment shall ever touch them.
In the eyes of the unwise, they did appear to die,
their going looked like a disaster,
their leaving us an annihilation;
but they are in peace.
Those who trust in him will understand the truth,
those who are faithful will live with him in love;
for grace and mercy await those he has chosen.

WISDOM 3:1-3,9

FOR DEEP HEALING

Lord, come into the deep heart of my mind. I want you to heal those things I have carried all this time. Take them to yourself; I cannot carry them any longer.

Ask Jesus to walk back through our lives and heal us. Find a quiet place. Come before him in humility and trust. Healing is an ever on-going process, so all problems will not be solved; but we can get the main barriers out of the way. Inner healing is accomplished when a past event no longer has power to hurt us, when it can be recalled without sadness, shame or guilt. Begin by saying:

Lord Jesus, thank you for being here, for your strength and presence. You can walk back through my life to the very moment when I was conceived. Help me even then; cleanse my bloodlines and free me from anything that may have caused difficulty before I was born, through my mother or circumstances . . . For this I give you thanks.

Heal me of the pain of birth . . . Thank you for being there to receive me into your arms when I was born. Consecrate me in that moment to you. I thank you, Jesus, for this has been done.

I praise you because in my infancy you were there, when I needed love, needed to be held close and comforted. Lord, do this in the depths of my being now . . . Fill in that part of me that was neglected with strong, fatherly love, security and strength . . . Thank you, Lord Jesus, for doing this.

Heal the part of my childhood that never felt wanted. Let me know that I am your child, a unique person in your family . . . Thank you.

Heal me of hurt in family relationships – a brother or sister who didn't understand. Help me to reach out in forgiveness to them and accept them . . . Thank you, Lord, for this that you have done.

Heal me of wounds and unkindnesses that I sustained at school . . . Take my classroom suffering, when I grew afraid to speak out because of ridicule or criticism . . . Open up that door in my heart; let me relate in groups to others, with confidence and courage to do what you call me to do . . . Thank you, Lord; I believe this is healed now.

Heal me of the experiences and fears I endured in adolescence. Transform all the things I did and had done for me, so that I can no longer remember them with shame . . . Thank you, Lord.

Heal me of my difficulties in my vocation in life: in marriage, hurts and sorrows . . . in religion, loneliness . . . Let me feel such strength of love pouring into me that I will never again doubt the path I am travelling is the one you called me to . . . Thank you, Lord.

Loneliness . . .
Rejection . . .
Abandonment . . .
Heal me of all these; of all the hurts that I have suffered in various situations; of the wrong that I have done, and the shame . . . help me to forgive myself and others . . .

Put in me a new sense of strength and purpose. Let me be a living witness to you.

As your love flows over me, I give you glory, Lord, because I know it is done.

> Now, be quiet for ten minutes; let the Spirit of God do his healing work in you, emptying your heart of everything that is not of God. Let God refill your heart with his love.

B. SCHLEMAN

A POEM

I look about me, sick and faint of soul:
The dwelling of God's glory is my goal.
But, though I look about so constantly,
No answer comes, none turns to rescue me.
Yet, as I wander through the grassy dale,
Or higher, as the mountain crags I scale,
Until alone on lonely peaks I gaze,
I grieve for having left my Saviour's ways.
And when I think how gentle is his touch,
And how his justice could demand so much,
My mind is changed, my labours seem the less,
And I regret my former foolishness.
Why should I rail on fortune or repine?
Why should I grieve God's remedy is mine.
Endure, then, as philosophers maintain
A brave man should, adversity and pain.

THOMAS BELSON
translated from the Latin by Michael Hodgetts

WITH GOD BY OUR SIDE

With God on our side who can be against us?
Since God did not spare his Son,
but gave him up to benefit us all,
we may be certain, after such a gift,
that he will not refuse anything he can give.
Nothing therefore can come between us and the
  love of Christ,
even if we are troubled or worried,
or being persecuted, or lacking food or clothes,
or being threatened or even attacked.
For I am certain of this:
neither death nor life,
no angel, no prince, nothing that exists,
nothing still to come,
not any power, or height or depth,
nor any created thing,
can ever come between us and the love of God
made visible in Christ Jesus our Lord.

ROMANS 8: 31-32,35,38-39

Chapter Seven

LOVE & FRIENDSHIP

DEEP WITHIN each one of us is the need to love and be loved The mystery and the joy of love is very close to the mystery and joy of God.

Let Us Love One Another

My dear people
let us love one another
since love comes from God
and everyone who loves is begotten by God
    and knows God.
Anyone who fails to love can never
    have known God,
because God is love.
God's love for us was revealed
when God sent into the world his only Son
so that we could have life through him;
this is the love I mean;
not our love for God,
but God's love for us
when he sent his Son
to be the sacrifice that takes our sins away.

I John 4:7-10

Love Is Not Just Words

If a man who was rich enough
    in this world's goods
saw that one of his brothers was in need,
but closed his heart to him,
how could the love of God be living in him?
My children,
our love is not to be just words or mere talk,
but something real and active;
only by this can we be certain
that we are children of the truth.

I John 3:17-19

FAITH, HOPE AND LOVE

Be ambitious for the higher gifts.
And I am going to show you a way
that is better than any of them.
If I have all the eloquence of men or of angels,
but speak without love,
I am simply a gong booming or a cymbal clashing.
Love is always patient and kind;
it is never jealous;
love is never boastful or conceited;
it is never rude or selfish;
it does not take offence, and is not resentful.
Love takes no pleasure in other people's sins
but delights in the truth;
it is always ready to excuse, to trust, to hope,
and to endure whatever comes.
There are three things that last:
faith, hope and love;
and the greatest of these is love.

I CORINTHIANS 12:31, 13:1,4-7,13.

THE GOOD SHEPHERD

I have come
so that they may have life
and have it to the full.
I am the good shepherd;
the good shepherd is one who lays down his life
    for his sheep.

JOHN 10: 10-11

YOUR HARD AND WAYWARD HEART

I come in little things,
Saith the Lord:
Yea! on the glancing wings
Of eager birds, the softly pattering feet
Of furred and gentle beasts, I come to meet
Your hard and wayward heart. In brown
   bright eyes
That peep from out of the brake, I stand confest.
On every nest
Where feathery Patience is content to brood
And leaves her pleasures for the high emprize
Of motherhood –
There doth my Godhead rest.

EVELYN UNDERHILL

LOVE

Love bade me welcome; yet my soul drew back,
   Guilty of dust and sin.
But quick-eyed Love, observing me grow slack
   From my first entrance in,
Drew nearer to me, sweetly questioning
   If I lacked anything.

'A guest,' I answered, 'worthy to be here.'
   Love said, 'You shall be he.'
'I, the unkind, ungrateful? Ah, my dear,
   I cannot look on thee.'
Love took my hand, and smiling did reply,
   'Who made the eyes but I?'

'Truth, Lord, but I have marred them;
    let my shame
  Go where it doth deserve.'
'And know you not,' says Love,
    'who bore the blame?'
  'My dear, then I will serve.'
'You must sit down,' says Love,
    'and taste my meat.'
  So I did sit and eat.

GEORGE HERBERT

FRIENDSHIP

Lord, when I am hungry
give me someone to feed;
when I am thirsty
give water for their thirst.
When I am sad
someone to lift from sorrow.
When burden weighs upon me
lay upon my shoulders
the burden of my fellows.
Lord, when I stand
greatly in need of tenderness,
give me someone who yearns
for love. May your will
be my bread; your grace
my strength; your love
my resting place.

FROM *Quaker Peace Service*

THE LOOK OF JESUS

In the Gospel according to Luke we read:

> But Peter said, 'Man, I do not know what you
> are talking about.' At that moment, while he
> was still speaking, a cock crew; and the Lord
> turned and looked straight at Peter . . . and
> Peter went outside and wept bitterly.

I had a fairly good relationship with the Lord.
I would ask him for things, converse with him,
praise him, thank him . . .

But always I had this uncomfortable feeling that
he wanted me to look at him. And I would not. I
would talk, but look away when I sensed he was
looking at me.

I was afraid I should find an accusation there of
some unrepented sin. I thought I should find a
demand there; there would be something he
wanted from me.

One day I finally summed up courage and looked!
There was no accusation. There was no demand.
The eyes just said, 'I love you.'

And I walked out and, like Peter, I wept.

ANTHONY DE MELLO

Chapter Eight

PRAISE & THANKSGIVING

THE MYSTERY of God is reflected in the wonder of this world, its beauty and power, yet it is fragile too. It can be the source of so much joy for us, and at the same time so easily be destroyed.

PROCLAIM YOUR PRAISE

I feel like singing this morning, O Lord.
I feel like telling everyone about me
    how great you are.
If only they could know the depths of your love
    and your eternal concern for those
        who will follow you!
But my songs are so often off-key.
My speech is so inadequate.
I simply cannot express what I feel,
    what I know to be true about your love
        for your creatures upon this world.

But even the songs of the birds
    proclaim your praises.
The heavens and the earth beneath them,
        the trees that reach towards you,
        the flowers that glow in colourful beauty,
        the green hills and soaring mountains,
        the valleys and the plains,
        the lakes and the rivers,
        the great oceans that pound our shores –
    they proclaim your greatness, O God,
        and your love for the children of men.

How glorious it is to be alive, O Lord!
May every breath of my body,
    every beat of my heart,
        be dedicated to your praise and glory.

PSALM 89 FROM *Psalms Now*

BLESSED BE GOD

Blessed be God the Father of our Lord Jesus Christ,
who has blessed us
with all the spiritual blessings of heaven in Christ.
Before the world was made,
he chose us, chose us in Christ,
to be holy and spotless,
and to live through love in his presence,
determining that we should become his
   adopted children,
through Jesus Christ,
for his own kind purposes.

EPHESIANS 1:3-5

THANKSGIVING FOR THE EARTH

God,
We thank you for this earth
which you have made full of riches.
We ask you to help us be good caretakers
   of your gifts.
Show us how to use our science and technology
   in creative, not destructive ways.
Help us to realise our relationships with all
   of your creation
so that the earth will always bring forth life
   to nourish us in body and spirit.
Through Christ
who died for all creation.

CAFOD

GOD'S GRANDEUR

The world is charged with the grandeur of God.
    It will flame out, like shining from shook foil;
    It gathers to a greatness, like the ooze of oil
Crushed. 'Why do men then now not reck his rod?
Generations have trod, have trod, have trod;
    And all is smeared with trade; bleared,
        smeared with toil;
    And wears man's smudge and share's man's
        smell: the soil
Is bare now, nor can foot feel, being shod.
And for all this, nature is never spent;
    There lives the dearest freshness deep down
        things;
And though the last lights off the black West went
    Oh, morning, at the brown brink eastward,
        springs –
Because the Holy Ghost over the bent
    World broods with warm breast and with ah!
        bright wings.

GERARD MANLEY HOPKINS

CLAP HANDS FOR JOY

    Clap your hands, stamp your feet!
Let your bodies and your voices explode with joy.
God is not some human concoction.
He is for real! And he is here!
Despite all attempts
        to rationalize him out of existence,
He is in our world,
    and he reigns over our universe.

PSALM 47

GLORIA

The whole world is full of glory:

Here is the glory of created things,
the earth and the sky,
the sun and the moon,
the stars and the vast expanses:

Here is fellowship
with all that was created,
the air and the wind,
cloud and rain,
sunshine and snow:

All life like the bubbling of a flowing river
and the dark currents of the depths of the sea
is full of glory.

The white waves of the breath of peace
on the mountains,
and the light striding
in the distances of the sea.

The explosion of the dawn wood-pigeons
and the fire of the sunset doves,
sheep and cattle at their grazing,
the joy of countless creeping things
as they blossom,
spider and ant
of nimble disposition
proclaim the riches of goodness.

BINSEY POPLARS
Felled 1879

My aspens dear, whose airy cages quelled,
Quelled or quenched in leaves the leaping sun,
All felled, felled, are all felled;
   Of a fresh and following folded rank
      Not spared, not one
      That dandled a sandalled
   Shadow that swam or sank
On meadow and river and wind-wandering
   weed-winding bank.

O if we but knew what we do
      When we delve or hew –
Hack and rack the growing green!
      Since country is so tender
To touch, her being so slender,
That, like this sleek and seeing ball
But a prick will make no eye at all,
Where we, even where we mean
      To mend her we end her,
   When we hew or delve:
After-comers cannot guess the beauty been.
Ten or twelve, only ten or twelve
   Strokes of havoc unselve
      The sweet especial scene,
   Rural scene, a rural scene,
   Sweet especial rural scene.

GERARD MANLEY HOPKINS

MORNING SONG

Morning, I greet you
dew-speckled and flower-crowned.
Cleanse me in the dawn.
Let me be rain-washed from night fears.
Open for me this day
as you open the rose.
I will unfurl in your light
and embrace your warmth.
Wind blow, and I will spin
dance-dazed through the day.

MARY JELF

Chapter Nine

JUSTICE & PEACE

THERE IS so much misery in our world, so much hunger and injustice, conflict and oppression. Often all we can do is to acknowledge the wrongs that are done and bring them to God. Sometimes, perhaps, we can do more.

LET THE OPPRESSED GO FREE

Is not this the sort of fast that pleases me –
it is the Lord Yahweh who speaks –
to break unjust fetters
and undo the thongs of the yoke,

to let the oppressed go free,
and break every yoke,
to share your bread with the hungry,
and shelter the homeless poor,

to clothe the man you see to be naked
and not turn from your own kin?
Then will your light shine like the dawn
and your wound be quickly healed over.

ISAIAH 58:6-8

PREPARATION FOR FINAL JUDGEMENT

Come, you whom my Father has blessed,
take for your heritage the kingdom
    prepared for you
since the foundation of the world.
For I was hungry and you gave me food;
I was thirsty and you gave me drink;
I was a stranger and you made me welcome;
naked and you clothed, sick and you visited me,
in prison and you came to see me.
Then the virtuous will say to him in reply,
'Lord, when did we see you hungry and feed you;
or thirsty and give you drink?
When did we see you a stranger
    and make you welcome;

naked and clothe you; sick or in prison
    and go to see you?'
And the king will answer, 'I tell you solemnly,
in so far as you did this to one of the least of these
    brothers of mine,
you did it to me.'

MATTHEW 25:34-40

FORGIVE US

Lord God almighty,
forgive your church
    its wealth among the poor,
    its fear among the unjust,
    its cowardice among the oppressed,
forgive us, your children,
    our lack of confidence in you,
    our lack of hope in your reign,
    our lack of faith in your presence,
    our lack of trust in your mercy.
Restore us to your covenant
    with your people;
    bring us to true repentance;
    teach us to accept the sacrifice of Christ;
    make us strong with the comfort of
        your Holy Spirit.
    Break us where we are proud,
    make us where we are weak,
    shame us where we trust ourselves,
    name us where we have lost ourselves;
through Jesus Christ our Lord. Amen.

CELEBRATING ONE WORLD

Are we so deaf
that we do not hear
a loving God warning us
that humanity is in danger
   of committing suicide?

Are we so selfish
that we do not hear
   the just God demanding
   that we do all we can
to stop injustice
suffocating the world
   and driving it to war?

Are we so alienated
that we can worship God
at ease in luxurious temples
which are often empty
in spite of all their liturgical pomp
and fail to see,
   hear
   and serve God
where he is present
and where he requires OUR presence
among humankind,
   the poor,
   the oppressed,
   the victims of injustice
in which we ourselves are often involved.

It is difficult
to do more than offer an emotional response,
    sorrow and regret.
It is even more difficult
to give up our comfort,
    break with old habits,
    let ourselves be moved by grace,
    and change our life,
– be converted.

DOM HELDA CAMARA

Chapter Ten

FORGIVENESS

DEEP DOWN, too, we all need forgiveness. Of ourselves first and then of one another, of what we do personally and of what is done in our name. Sometimes the hardest act of all is to forgive ourselves.

GOD IS GOODNESS

And thus throughout this vision I was obliged
    to see and know that we are sinners
and do many evil things that we ought
    to leave undone
and leave many good deeds undone
    that we ought to do.
Therefore we deserve pain and anger.
Notwithstanding all this I saw unequivocally
    that our Lord was never angry
nor ever shall be, for he is God:
    Good, Life, Truth, Love, Peace.
His love and his unity do not allow him
    to be angry.
For I saw truly that it was against the nature
    of his wisdom
and against the nature of his goodness.
God is the goodness that may not be angry
    for he is nothing else but goodness.

JULIAN OF NORWICH

CALL TO REPENTANCE

'But now, now – it is Yahweh who speaks –
come back to me with all your heart,
fasting, weeping, mourning.'
Let your hearts be broken, not your garments torn,
turn to Yahweh your God again,
for he is all tenderness and compassion,
slow to anger, rich in graciousness,
and ready to relent.

JOEL 2:12-13

THE JOY OF BEING FORGIVEN

What are you looking for in this church?
What are you doing here?
Are you ready – in the blunt biblical phrase –
to 'do the truth'?
Do not mix up shame and sin,
or your faults and your guilt feelings,
or repentance and remorse.
Be reconciled to yourself.
Forgive . . . yourself.
Let joy be unconfined . . .
Christ is saving you.

P. TALEC

GOD LOVES YOU

You are God' s chosen race, his saints;
he loves you,
and you should be clothed with sincere
    compassion,
in kindness and humility,
gentleness and patience.
Bear with one another;
forgive each other as soon as a quarrel begins.
The Lord has forgiven you;
    now you must do the same.
Over all these clothes, to keep them together
    and complete them,
put on love.

COLOSSIANS 3:12-14

KINDNESS

The Pharisees said to his disciples,
'Why does your master eat with tax collectors
    and sinners?'
When Jesus heard this he replied,
'It is not the healthy who need the doctor,
but the sick.
Go and learn the meaning of the words:
What I want is mercy, not sacrifice.
And indeed I did not come to call the virtuous,
but sinners.'

MATTHEW 9:11-13

THE LOST SHEEP

What man among you with a hundred sheep,
    losing one,
would not leave the ninety-nine in the wilderness
and go after the missing one till he found it?
And when he found it,
would he not joyfully take it on his shoulders
and then, when he got home,
call together his friends and neighbours?
'Rejoice with me,' he would say,
'I have found my sheep that was lost.'
In the same way, I tell you,
there will be more rejoicing in heaven over
    one repentant sinner
than over ninety-nine virtuous men
who have no need of repentance.

LUKE 15:4-7

LEFT BY THE BODY OF A CHILD IN THE WOMEN'S CONCENTRATION CAMP AT RAVENSBRUCK

O Lord, remember not only the men and women
    of good will,
but also those of ill will.
But do not remember all the suffering
    they have inflicted on us;
remember the fruits we have bought,
    thanks to this suffering –
our comradeship, our loyalty, our humility,
    our courage, our generosity,
the greatness of heart which has grown
    out of all this,
and when they come to judgement,
    let all the fruits which we have borne
    be their forgiveness.

QUOTED BY MARY CRAIG IN *Blessings*

FORGIVE EACH OTHER

Father, we know that you wish us
    to forgive each other.
Help us to forgive and to be forgiven.
Take away from our hearts feelings of resentment.
Teach us to be truly merciful,
and deserving of mercy from you
and from others.
Amen.

FORGIVE MY SINS

O God, have mercy!
I know my guilt is great.
Look upon my emptiness and loneliness,
　　consider kindly my afflictions and despair,
　　remember the perpetual presence
　　　of my human weaknesses and instincts.
Regard once more the pernicious
　　　and violent forces
　　that oppose your will in my life;
Forgive me my many sins,
　　and restore me to yourself.
Watch over me and hold on to me, O God,
　　lest I fall again.

PSALM 25 FROM *Psalms Now*

Chapter Eleven

BEING A CHRISTIAN

BEING A christian means, among other things, wanting to know God. But it also means bearing witness to Jesus Christ, trying to live a life of love based on the gospels.

A CREED FROM INDIA

I believe in one world, full of riches meant
    for everyone to enjoy;
I believe in one race, the family of humankind,
    learning how to live together by the hard way
    of self-sacrifice.
I believe in one life, exciting and positive;
    which enjoys all the beauty, integrity
    and science;
    uses the discipline of work to enrich society;
    harmonizes with the life of Jesus,
    and develops into a total joy.
I believe in one morality: love –
    the holiness of sharing the sorrow and joys
      of others;
    bringing together people as true friends;
    working to rid the world of the root causes
    of poverty and injustice, ignorance and fear;
love, the test of all my thoughts and motives;
love, guiding me, controlling me, assuring me of
    God's forgiveness;
    and giving me confidence under
    his Spirit's control.
I believe in Jesus, and the Bible's evidence
    about him;
    whose life, death and resurrection prove God's
    lasting love for the world;
    who combines in himself, life, love, truth,
    humanity, reality
    and God;
    who saves, guides and unites all people who
    follow his way.

I believe in the purpose of God,
    to unite in Christ everything, spiritual
        or secular,
    to renew society, individuals and nations,
    and to guide all governments under his fatherly
        direction.

FROM *Confessing our Faith around the World*

OPEN MY EYES

Open my eyes that they may see
the deepest needs of men and women;

Move my hands that they may feed
the hungry;

Touch my heart that it may bring warmth
to the despairing;

Teach me the generosity
that welcomes strangers;

Let me share my possessions
to clothe the naked;

Give me the care
that strengthens the sick;

Make me share in the quest
to set the prisoners free;

In sharing our anxieties and our love,
our poverty and our prosperity,
we partake of your divine presence.

CANAAN BANANA (ZIMBABWE)

HELPING OTHERS

Pure, unspoilt religion,
in the eyes of God our Father is this:
coming to the help of orphans and widows
when they need it,
and keeping oneself
uncontaminated by the world.

JAMES I:27

FOLLOW JESUS

If anyone wants to be a follower of mine,
let him renounce himself and take up his cross
    and follow me.
For anyone who wants to save their life
    will lose it;
but anyone who loses their life for my sake
    will find it.

MATTHEW 16:24-25

LIVE IN FAITH

I have been crucified with Christ,
and I live now not with my own life
but with the life of Christ who lives in me.
The life I now live in this body
I live in faith: faith in the Son of God
    who loved me
and who sacrificed himself for my sake.

GALATIANS 2:20

CARING FOR THE SUFFERING

On the street I saw a naked child, hungry and shivering in the cold. I became angry and said to God, 'Why do you permit this? Why don't you do something?'

For a while God said nothing. That night he replied, quite suddenly, 'I certainly did something. I made you.'

ANTHONY DE MELLO

A LIGHT FOR OTHERS

I have made you a light for the nations
so that my salvation
may reach the ends of the earth.

ACTS 13: 47

LIVING BY EXAMPLE

When he had washed their feet
   and put on his clothes again
he went back to the table.
'Do you understand' he said 'what I have
   done to you?
You call me Master and Lord, and rightly; so I am.
If I, then, the Lord and Master, have washed
   your feet,
you should wash each other's feet.
I have given you an example so that you may copy
   what I have done to you.'

JOHN 13: 12-15

PRAISE GOD

The faithful all lived together
and owned everything in common;
they sold their goods and possessions
and shared out the proceeds amongst themselves
according to what each one needed.
They went as a body to the Temple every day
but met in their houses for the breaking
    of the bread;
they shared their food gladly and generously;
they praised God and were looked up to
    by everyone.

ACTS 2:44-47

AMBASSADORS FOR CHRIST

For anyone who is in Christ,
    there is a new creation;
the old creation has gone,
    and now the new one is here.
It is all God's work.
It was God who reconciled us to himself
    through Christ
and gave us the work of handing on
    this reconciliation.
In other words, God in Christ was reconciling
    the world to himself,
not holding men's faults against them,
and he has entrusted to us the news
    that they are reconciled.
So we are ambassadors for Christ

2 CORINTHIANS 5:17-20

TEST YOURSELF

Examine yourselves to make sure
  you are in the faith;
test yourselves.
Do you acknowledge that Jesus Christ
  is really in you?
If not, you have failed the test.

2 CORINTHIANS 13: 5-6

ATTAIN SALVATION

Now there is but one possible way
  for a man to attain to salvation.
There is not one for the Jew, another for the
  Christian and a third for the heathen.
No! God is one, human nature is one,
  salvation is one
and the way to it is one;
and that is the desire of the soul
  turned towards God.
When the desire is alive and breaks forth
  in any creature under heaven,
then the lost sheep is found and the shepherd
  has it on his shoulder.

WILLIAM LAW

ACT JUSTLY

What is good has been explained to you,
this is what Yahweh asks of you:
only this, to act justly,
to love tenderly
and to walk humbly with your God.

MICAH 6:8

WHAT THE WORLD EXPECTS OF CHRISTIANS

For a long time during those frightful years
(during the occupation of France) I waited for a
great voice to speak up in Rome. I, an unbeliever?
Precisely. For I knew that the spirit would be
lost if it did not utter a cry of condemnation
when faced with force.

What the world expects of christians is that
they should speak out, loud and clear, and
that they should voice their condemnation in
such a way that never a doubt, never the
slightest doubt, could arise in the heart of the
simplest person. That they should get away
from abstractions and confront the blood-stained
face history has taken on today. The grouping
we need is a grouping of people resolved
to speak out clearly and to pay up personally.

It may be . . . that christianity will insist on
maintaining a compromise, or else on giving its
condemnations the obscure form of the
encyclical. Perhaps it will insist on losing once
and for all the virtue of revolt and indignation
that belonged to it long ago.

I can only speak of what I know.
And what I know is that if christians made up
their minds to it, millions of voices – millions
I say – throughout the world would be added
to the appeal of a handful of isolated
individuals who, without any sort of
affiliation, today intercede almost everywhere
and ceaselessly for children and for all.

ALBERT CAMUS *Resistance, Rebellion and Death*

Chapter Twelve

FAITH & REDEMPTION

IT IS IMPOSSIBLE to hope for what we know to be certain. Yet hope and faith combine to make acceptable whatever the future may bring.

HOPE

To hope means to be ready
at every moment
for that which is not yet born,
and yet not become desperate
if there is no birth in our lifetime.
There is no sense in hoping
for that which already exists
or for that which cannot be.
Those whose hope is weak
settle down for comfort or for violence;
those whose hope is strong
see and cherish all signs of new life
and are ready every moment
to help the birth
of that which is ready to be born.

ERICH FROMM

DOING YOUR WILL

O God of mercy,
You know the secrets of my heart
    and the desires of my flesh.
You know I want so much to do your will.
You know my greatest enemy is myself,
    how ineffectual I am
        in dealing with my inner conflicts.
You know, and you have assured me that you care.
You have judged my wickedness;
    now rise up to deliver me
        from its ugly consequences.

PSALM 7 FROM *Psalms Now*

A Dawn out of Darkness

You will forget your sufferings,
remember them as waters that have passed away.
Your life, more radiant than the noonday,
will make a dawn of darkness.
Full of hope, you will live secure,
dwelling well and safely guarded.

Job 11:16-18

A More Powerful Force

It is an ironic fact in this nuclear age,
when the horizon of human knowledge
and human experience
has passed far beyond any
that any age has ever known,
that we turn back at this time
to the older source of wisdom and strength,
to the Lords of the prophets and the saints,
who tell us that faith is more powerful
    than doubt,
that hope is more potent than despair,
and that only through the love
that is sometimes called charity
can we conquer those forces
within ourselves
and throughout all the world
that threaten the very existence of mankind.

John F. Kennedy

GIVE US HOPE

Give us hope to look forward to a happy tomorrow.
Give us courage to face the hardships without
    losing hope.
Give us faith so that the joy of receiving Christ
    will lead us to serve others.
Give us appreciation for the gifts we have received
that we might use them responsibly, daring to give
friendship, service, and love.
Give us Christmas throughout the year.

FROM *Christian Conference of Asia*

THE WHEEL OF THE LAW

The wheel of the law turns without pause.

After rain, good weather
in the wink of an eye.

The universe throws off its muddy clothes.

For ten thousand miles
the landscape
spreads out like a beautiful brocade,
light breezes, smiling flowers.

High in the trees, amongst
the sparkling leaves
all the birds sing at once.
Man and animals rise up reborn.

What could be more natural?
After sorrow, comes happiness.

A PRAYER FROM VIETNAM

A DECLARATION OF FAITH

We believe in God the Father
who created all the world,
who will unite all things in Christ
and who wants all people to live together
as brothers and sisters in one family.

We believe in God the Son
who became man, died, and rose in triumph,
to reconcile all the world to God,
to break down every separating barrier
of race, culture or class,
and to unite all people into one body.

He is exalted as Lord over all,
the only Lord over every area of our life.
He summons both the individual and society,
both the Church and the State,
to seek reconciliation and unity between all
and justice and freedom for all.

We believe in God the Spirit,
the pledge of God's coming reign
who gives the Church power to proclaim the good
news to all the world,
to love and serve all people,
to strive for justice and peace,
to warn that God judges both
the individual and the Nation,
and to summon all the world to accept God's reign
here and now.
FROM *Confessing our Faith Around the World*

THE TRUTH

We know the truth,
not only by the reason,
but by the heart.

BLAISE PASCAL

HOPE FOR GRACE AND GLORY

My God, I hope in you, for grace and for glory,
because of your promises, your mercy
and power.

THE HAND OF GOD

And I said to the man who stood at the gate of the
year:
    'Give me a light that I may tread safely into the
    unknown'.
And he replied:
    'Go out into the darkness and put your hand
    into the hand of God. That shall be to you better
    than light and safer than a known way.'
So I went forth, and finding the hand of God, trod
gladly into the night. And he led me towards the
hills and the breaking of the day in the lone East.

M. L. HASKINS

Acknowledgements

The publishers wish to express their gratitude to the following for permission to use copyright material:

Ateliers et Presses de Taizé, F-71250 Taizé Communauté, France for the prayer by Brother Roger.

CAFOD for extracts from *Celebrating One World*.

Concordia Publishing House for extracts from *Psalms Now* © 1973 by Leslie F. Brandt.

Darton Longman & Todd Ltd for all bible quotations which are taken from the *Jerusalem Bible* © 1966, 1967 and 1968 by Darton Longman and Todd Ltd and Doubleday & Co Ltd. Also for extracts from *Catholic Prayer Book* © 1987 by Anthony Bullen.

M. Cynthia Davies for the poems *The Christ of Nature* and *Life is Greater than Death* (translations) which first appeared in *A Welsh Pilgrim's Manual* 1989, published by Gomer Press.

HarperCollins Publishers for *The Authentic Human Being* by Archbishop Romero from *The Church is All of Us*.

Mary Jelf for *More Thoughts on the Tube*, *We Are No Longer Alone* and *Morning Song*.

Mambo Press, Zimbabwe for *Open my Eyes* by Canaan S. Banana for *The Gospel According to the Ghetto*.

McCrimmon Publishing Co Ltd, Great Wakering, Essex for extracts from *Prayers for the Depressed* by Michael Hollings.

Octopus Publishing Group Library for extract from *The Velveteen Rabbit* by Margery Williams, published by William Heinemann Ltd.

St Paul Publications for extracts from *Fifty Prayers Young People* by A. Bullen.

Sheed and Ward for *Are we so deaf* by Dom Helda Camara.

The Sovereign Military Order of Malta for extracts from *Prayer of the Sovereign Military Order of Malta* (1989)

SPCK for extracts from *The Wisdom of the English Mystics* (1978) by Thomas Traherne.

WCC Publications, Geneva for extracts from *Why O Lord? Psalms and Sermons from Namibia* 1986 by Zephania Kameeta, and *Jesus Christ, the Life of the World, A Worship Book* (No. 35) 1983.